The Power *of*
THINKING BIG

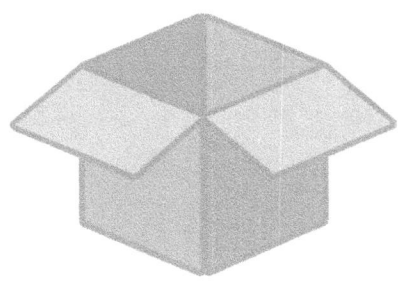

Devotionals of Wisdom to Inspire
Bigger and Bolder Thoughts

RACINE, WI

The Power of Thinking Big
ISBN: 979-8-88898-168-9 - *Paperback*
ISBN: 979-8-88898-169-6 - *Hardcover*
ISBN: 979-8-88898-170-2 - *Ebook*
Copyright © 2025 by John C. Maxwell & Honor Books, Racine, WI

Cover design and manuscript by Faille Schmitz.

INTRODUCTION

Mark Twain once said, "Take your mind out every now and then and dance on it. It is getting all caked up." That was his way of saying, "Try something new, break new ground, get out of your rut."

This is good advice for all of us. Sometimes we need something to jolt us out of a lifeless routine — a bold new thought, a different slant on a familiar subject, or a bit of wisdom from someone who's "walked down that road" before we have.

The quotes in this book have been selected to inspire you to see life from a different angle. Many contain a little barb or twist to get your attention. Some will make you laugh; others will make you think — think big! I hope that they will equip you to make your world better tomorrow than it is today.

After all, you never know when you will discover that big thought that will change your life!

JOHN C. MAXWELL

SERENITY

What you're supposed to do when you don't like a thing is change it. If you can't change it, change the way you think about it. Don't complain.

MAYA ANGELOU

This wisdom is a great recipe for an effective, yet satisfied life. There are plenty of circumstances in life that we cannot change, not overnight at the very least. How does stewing on such things serve you? It takes discernment to know the difference between what you can and cannot change, but dwelling on either with a negative mindset can sour your present and fog up your vision of the future.

Thinking in its lower grades is comparable to paper money, and in its higher forms it is a kind of poetry.

HAVELOCK ELLIS

Watch your life and doctrine closely. Persevere in them, because if you do, you will save both yourself and your hearers.

1 TIMOTHY 4:16 NIV

Every person who has become successful has simply formed the habit of doing things that failures dislike doing and will not do.

JOHN C. MAXWELL

POWER UP

What is something you've been tolerating that is within your power to change?

KEEP THE DREAM ALIVE

Never let go of a dream until you're ready to wake up and make it happen.

In tough times, sometimes a dream is all that keeps you going. The belief that the future holds great things in store for you makes life colorful. Dreams are gifts from God—seeds of purpose planted in the soil of our hearts. But they're not meant to stay in our sleep; they're meant to be lived out. All you have to do is keep moving toward it, taking the necessary baby steps to accomplish what you set out to do. God honors those who don't just dream big, but act boldly.

It takes all the running you can do to keep in the same place. If you want to get somewhere else, you must run at least twice as fast as that!

THE QUEEN OF HEARTS IN ALICE IN WONDERLAND

Blessed is the one who perseveres under trial because, having stood the test, that person will receive the crown of life that the Lord has promised to those who love him.

JAMES 1:12 NIV

Practice doesn't make perfect—it makes permanent.

JOHN C. MAXWELL

POWER UP

What dream have you been sleeping on?

_____

_____

_____

_____

_____

ALL HEART

Our hearts are often revealed in times of testing. When we're called upon to step up to the plate, it's our hearts shining through our response that can make or break the outcome. Whether you're leading, serving, creating, or simply showing up in daily life, it's the depth of your love, the sincerity of your faith, and the purity of your motives that God honors and inspires others.

One difference between perseverance and obstinacy is that one often comes from a strong will, and the other from a strong won't.

HENRY WAR BEECHER

"I the Lord search the heart and examine the mind, to reward each person according to their conduct, according to what their deeds deserve."

JEREMIAH 17:10 NIV

Your attitude is either your best friend or your worst enemy, your greatest asset or your greatest liability.

JOHN C. MAXWELL

POWER UP

What is the condition of your heart in the things you pursue?

POSITIVE REINFORCEMENT

*Don't just learn something from every experience;
learn something positive.*

ALLEN H. NEUHARTH

Everyone who has successfully trained a pet knows this effective learning technique: positive reinforcement. Trainers use rewards and audible affection to affirm their animals when they perform the correct action. In a similar way, don't beat yourself down with what you could have handled better, but train yourself to highlight the positives.

When you're through changing, you're through.

BRUCE BARTON

. . . the goodness of God leadeth thee to repentance . . .

ROMANS 2:4

*People are changed, not by coercion or intimidation,
but by example.*

JOHN C. MAXWELL

POWER UP

*Do you tend to find yourself dwelling on the negative
or do you have an eye for silver lining?*

SWEAT EQUITY

There are no shortcuts to anyplace worth going.

BEVERLY SILLS

Nothing good in life comes easy. As much as we might lament difficulties, it is inevitable that we will encounter them. A person with an attitude that is ready to roll up their sleeves to overcome an obstacle will achieve more than someone trying to find the easy way around. Even if you trip over it in the process, you'll approach the next one as a wiser person. With time, you'll find yourself strengthened and equipped to handle situations that would've been daunting when you first started out, and goals that used to be dreams become visible on the horizon.

Lazy hands make for poverty, but diligent hands bring wealth.

PROVERBS 10:4 NIV

Stop trying to grow your organization. Work on people's attitudes. If you do that, your organization will experience 10 percent growth overnight.

JOHN C. MAXWELL

One definition of insanity is to believe that you can keep doing what you've been doing and get different results.

POWER UP

What obstacle are you facing right now?

POSITIVE PLANNING

> *It pays to plan ahead. It wasn't raining when Noah built the ark.*

Life can be unpredictable. Some things happen that we never saw coming, but many can be smoothed over by being properly prepared. Am I saying you should have a stockpile of food and weapons in the event of a zombie apocalypse? No. But basic preparations such as putting a little money away every month, caring for your body with a healthy diet and exercise, and investing time regularly into your relationship with God will cover most situations. Believe for the best, but prepare for the worst.

I not only use all the brains I have, but all I can borrow.

WOODROW WILSON

And we know that all things work together for good to them that love God, to them who are the called according to his purpose.

ROMANS 8:28

Leadership determines the direction of the company. Organization determines the potential of the company. Personnel determine the success of the company.

JOHN C. MAXWELL

POWER UP

What are some plans you would benefit from putting in place now?

MAKE IT HAPPEN

Ideas won't keep: something must be done about them.

ALFRED NORTH WHITEHEAD

An idea is a great thing. A good idea represents hope for the future and a dream to put a fire in your belly, but it is a spark that requires effort to fan into flame. Whether it's a God-given vision, a stirring in your heart, or a solution to a problem, ideas require courage, discipline, and faith to become reality. If you have an idea you really believe in, commit to it and make it happen!

*You've got to get up every morning with determination if
you're going to go to bed with satisfaction.*

GEORGE HORACE LORIMER

*Do not merely listen to the word, and so deceive yourselves.
Do what it says.*

JAMES 1:22 NIV

Pay now, play later; play now, pay later.

JOHN C. MAXWELL

POWER UP

When was the last time you stepped out in a big way for a new idea?

WHEN REST
BECOMES RUST

---

*The best cure for a sluggish mind
is to disturb its routine.*

WILLIAM H. DANFORTH

Comfort is a curious thing. It fuels the drive of many to work for a "comfortable" lifestyle of a nice home, lavish vacations, and first-class tickets. At the same time, it can enable a stagnant life of mediocrity. Stagnancy breeds laziness and dulls your shine. It's when we step out of our comfort zone that growth happens. The first step is the hardest, but it is a worthy investment in your future.

He who is good at making excuses is seldom good for anything else.

BENJAMIN FRANKLIN

I went by the field of the slothful, and by the vineyard of the man void of understanding; and, lo, it was all grown over with thorns, and nettles had covered the face thereof, and the stone wall thereof was broken down.

PROVERBS 24:30-31

We first form habits. Then habits form us.

JOHN C. MAXWELL

POWER UP

In what aspect of your life has comfort bred stagnancy?

VICTIM OR VICTOR

Most people want to change the world to improve their lives. What a wasted effort. If they would only improve themselves, they would be better off and so would the world.

Small minds point the blame for their problems at anyone or anything but themselves. While we are subject to many factors beyond our control, we have the choice to live our lives as victims or victors. It's easier to point fingers than to look inward, but lasting impact comes from people who let God refine their character, attitudes, and actions. Take accountability, don't let the past define your future, and take ownership of your life—you only have one.

In youth we want to change the world.
In old age we want to change the youth.

GARTH HENRICHS

"How can you say to your brother, 'Let me take the speck out of your eye,' when all the time there is a plank in your own eye? You hypocrite, first take the plank out of your own eye, and then you will see clearly to remove the speck from your brother's eye."

MATTHEW 7:4-5 NIV

People stop growing when the price gets too high.

JOHN C. MAXWELL

POWER UP

Search your heart—is there any area of your life you've been shirking responsibility for?

_____

_____

_____

_____

_____

YOUR LIFE IS A GARDEN

> *The richest soil, uncultivated,*
> *produces the rankest weeds.*
>
> **PLUTARCH**

Every person's life is their own patch of soil. A gardener envisions an array of flowers, a farmer envisions a bountiful crop—whatever dream God has given you, your life is your plot of land to cultivate it. However, potential amounts to nothing if you don't put in the elbow grease to bring it to fruition. So put on your gloves and work the soil of your life with diligence and integrity.

Whoever walks in integrity walks securely, but whoever takes crooked paths will be found out.

PROVERBS 10:9 NIV

Image is what people think we are.
Integrity is what we really are.

JOHN C. MAXWELL

Any time the going seems easier, better check and see if you're not going downhill.

POWER UP

What are you growing in the garden of your life?

_____

_____

_____

_____

_____

TRAILBLAZING

Every generation needs a new revolution.

THOMAS JEFFERSON

"This is the way we've always done it" is a statement that causes great discomfort in the hearts and minds of free thinkers. Tradition has enormous value when accompanied by reason, but riding on the coattails of the previous generation can stagnate growth and innovation. If you have a vision, don't be afraid to divert from the beaten path to blaze your own trail.

If you're not doing something with your life,
it doesn't matter how long it is.

PEACE CORPS COMMERCIAL

For what shall it profit a man, if he shall gain the whole
world, and lose his own soul?

MARK 8:36

If your vision doesn't cost you something, it's a daydream.

JOHN C. MAXWELL

POWER UP

What "path less travelled" has been calling you lately?

_____

_____

_____

_____

_____

EXCUSES, EXCUSES

When you find yourself wanting to dodge commitments you've made, it's worth taking an honest inward look at why. Are you stretched too thin? Did you feel pressured to take on the role? Or is the desire to escape coming from a place of fear or laziness? Jesus says in Matthew 5, "*But let your 'Yes' be 'Yes,' and your 'No,' 'No.'*" Whatever reasoning you can dig up, conduct yourself with integrity. Discern whether you need to learn to protect your rest and learn to say "no", or make a shift in attitude and discipline.

Ninety-nine percent of failures come from people who have the habit of making excuses.

GEORGE WASHINGTON CARVER

You were taught, with regard to your former way of life, to put off your old self, which is being corrupted by its deceitful desires; to be made new in the attitude of your minds . . .

EPHESIANS 4:22-23 NIV

Our attitude at the beginning of a task will affect its outcome more than anything else.

JOHN C. MAXWELL

POWER UP

What excuses have been holding you back lately?

LIFE UNFILTERED

In this internet age where there is more pressure than ever to construct a perfect image online, people deeply crave authenticity. It is easy to post a filtered vacation photo with an inspirational caption. But when someone invites you into their life and their conduct in the day-to-day proves them the real deal, that is where true admiration grows. Who you are in the rawness and realness of life is what will really make an impression on those around you.

Our strength is seen in the things we stand for; our weakness is seen in the things we fall for.

THEODORE EPP

. . . keeping a clear conscience, so that those who speak maliciously against your good behavior in Christ may be ashamed of their slander.

1 PETER 3:16 NIV

If people respect you but don't like you, they won't stay with you. If they like you but don't respect you, they'll stay with you, but they won't follow you. To be an effective leader, you must earn both from your people.

JOHN C. MAXWELL

POWER UP

What filters do you place on yourself for others?
What would happen if you took them down?

PURPOSE OVER PESSIMISM

> *One-fifth of the people are against everything all the time.*
>
> ROBERT KENNEDY

I n a world where negativity often shouts louder than hope, it's easy to feel discouraged by constant criticism or opposition. That doesn't mean we should let resistance dim our light. Jesus faced opposition at every turn, yet He moved forward in love, truth, and purpose. Staying focused on what and who we are living for is like the guiding light of a lighthouse in a storm.

I am only one, but I am one. I cannot do everything, but I can do something. And that which I can do, by the grace of God, I will do.

DWIGHT L. MOODY

Now the God of patience and consolation grant you to be like-minded one toward another according to Christ Jesus . . .

ROMANS 15:5

Your attitude is the eye of your soul. If your attitude is negative, then you see things negatively. If it's positive, then you see things positively.

JOHN C. MAXWELL

POWER UP

Are you a pessimist, a realist, or an optimist?

_____

_____

_____

_____

_____

TRUST THE PROCESS

We judge ourselves by what we feel capable of doing; others judge us by what we have done.

HENRY WADSWORTH LONGFELLOW

Often, we carry dreams, callings, and capacities in our hearts that others may not yet see. But God sees both who we are and who we are becoming. While the world may measure us by results, God measures us by faith, obedience, and the willingness to take the next step. Don't be discouraged if your actions haven't caught up with your aspirations yet. God's idea of productivity is not human productivity — keep moving forward and trust in His timing.

And whosoever shall exalt himself shall be abased; and he that shall humble himself shall be exalted.

MATTHEW 23:12

You cannot go any higher than your self-image.

JOHN C. MAXWELL

It's right to be content with what you have, never with what you are.

POWER UP

What area of your life have you been investing in, but have yet to see fruit?

A DARING FAITH

This wholehearted faith is the essence of the missionary. It's the kind of bold surrender that does not shy away from God's calling and refuses to run when things get hard. Following Him requires courage to give our all, persistence to keep going, and trust that every step in obedience has eternal purpose. When we live this way we may not always be comfortable, but we will always be in the center of God's will. And there is no safer, more fulfilling place to be.

. . . in all these things we are more than conquerors through him that loved us.

ROMANS 8:37

A difficult crisis can be more readily endured if we retain the conviction that our existence holds a purpose—a cause to pursue, a person to love, a goal to achieve.

JOHN C. MAXWELL

Never retreat in the face of difficulties. Advance as conditions permit. If conditions don't permit, create those conditions.

POWER UP

What step of faith have you been debating on taking?

DON'T POSTPONE BLESSING

Before putting off until tomorrow something you can do today, study it closely. Maybe you can postpone it indefinitely.

How often do we delay the promptings of God, waiting for a more convenient moment that never comes? Scripture urges, *"Today, if you hear His voice, do not harden your hearts"* (Hebrews 3:15). Whether it is a demanding role you're taking on, a spiritual challenger, or simply a chore, God rewards diligence at every scale. Trust that whatever God places on your plate today, He will empower you to begin with His blessing.

Don't put off for tomorrow what you can do today, because if you enjoy it today, you can do it again tomorrow.

JAMES A. MICHENER

Diligent hands will rule, but laziness ends in forced labor.

PROVERBS 12:24 NIV

A procrastinator puts off until tomorrow the things he has already put off until today.

JOHN C. MAXWELL

POWER UP

Is there a prompting of God that you have been brushing off?

_____

_____

_____

_____

_____

LOAVES AND FISHES

God rarely waits for perfect conditions to do a perfect work, He simply looks for a willing heart. Throughout Scripture God used what was already in people's hands—Moses' staff, David's sling—not because they were impressive, but because they were available. Don't let time pass needlessly waiting for the right moment or the right feeling. Turning small steps of faith into big impact is God's specialty.

When you cease to make a contribution, you begin to die.

ELEANOR ROOSEVELT

The wise store up choice food and olive oil,
but fools gulp theirs down.

PROVERBS 21:20 NIV

The true test of stewardship is not what your money
is doing for you but what it's doing to you.

JOHN C. MAXWELL

POWER UP

Name a simple step of faith you could take in the coming week.

RISK AND REGRET

Safe living generally makes for regrets later on.

Playing it safe may feel secure, but it often leads to missed opportunities and unfulfilled callings. God rarely calls us to comfort—He calls us to courage. Abraham left everything familiar, Peter stepped out of the boat, and Esther risked her life to save her people. When we trust God enough to step beyond the familiar, we discover that His plans are far greater than our own—and we live with purpose, not regret.

You miss 100 percent of the shots you never take.

WAYNE GRETZKY

The wicked flee though no one pursues,
but the righteous are as bold as a lion.

PROVERBS 28:1 NIV

The greatest mistake we make is living in constant fear
that we will make one.

JOHN C. MAXWELL

POWER UP

Is there shot you wish you would have taken in the past?
How has that experience influenced your decision-making today?

_____

_____

_____

_____

_____

DREAM BIG

Make no small plans, for they have no capacity to stir men's souls.

God is not a God of small dreams — He's the Creator of the universe and the One who places divine purpose in human hearts. Scripture tells us, "*Now to him who is able to do immeasurably more than all we ask or imagine…*" (Ephesians 3:20). Don't shrink back from big dreams because they seem impossible. Dare to dream God-sized dreams, and trust Him to awaken souls — starting with your own.

The future belongs to people who see possibilities before they become obvious.

TED LEVITT

But Jesus beheld them, and said unto them, "With men this is impossible; but with God all things are possible."

MATTHEW 19:26

Problems are those things we see when we take our eyes off the goal.

JOHN C. MAXWELL

POWER UP

What's your big dream?

_____

_____

_____

_____

_____

KEEP MOVING FORWARD

I will go anywhere as long as it's forward.

DAVID LIVINGSTONE

God's call is always forward — toward growth, sanctification, and deeper trust in Him. The Apostle Paul captured this mindset when he wrote, *"Forgetting what is behind and straining toward what is ahead, I press on toward the goal…"* (Philippians 3:13–14). Whether the path is clear or uncertain, we can move boldly knowing God goes with us. Today, resist the urge to stay stuck in what was, and take the next step into what could be.

The man who starts out going nowhere,
generally gets there.

DALE CARNEGIE

Where there is no vision, the people perish:
but he that keepeth the law, happy is he.

PROVERBS 29:18

Vision adds value to everything.

JOHN C. MAXWELL

POWER UP

What typically trips you up from moving forward?

A BLESSING IN DISGUISE

> *Opportunities are seldom labeled.*
>
> JOHN A. SHEDD

The doors God opens often don't come with flashing signs or perfect conditions — they come disguised as interruptions, challenges, or small beginnings. It takes spiritual attentiveness to recognize that what looks ordinary may actually be divine. When our ears are tuned to God's voice, recognizing His whispered invitations into faith becomes easier.

Be very careful, then, how you live—not as unwise but as wise, making the most of every opportunity . . .

EPHESIANS 5:15-16 NIV

What I perceive . . . determines what I receive . . . which determines how I achieve.

JOHN C. MAXWELL

The desire for safety stands against every great and noble enterprise.

POWER UP

What blessing have you uncovered in an unlikely disguise in the past?

DUE DILIGENCE

In a world that often rewards shortcuts and excuses, God calls us to walk in excellence and honesty. When we do things the right way—not just the fast or easy way—we honor God, build trust, and cultivate character. Choose the path of diligence and truth. It may cost more effort now, but it saves the weight of regret later and brings glory to the One you serve.

Between saying and doing,
many a pair of shoes is worn out.

ITALIAN PROVERB

Do not merely listen to the word,
and so deceive yourselves. Do what it says.

JAMES 1:22 NIV

People do what people see. They forget your words
but follow your footsteps.

JOHN C. MAXWELL

POWER UP

What area of your life could do with a boost in diligence?

_____

_____

_____

_____

_____

COURAGE TO CHANGE

If you want to make enemies, try to change something.

WOODROW WILSON

Real change, especially the kind God calls us to, often disrupts comfort zones and challenges the status quo. Whether it's standing for truth, pursuing justice, or simply choosing a new path of obedience, not everyone will cheer you on. Courageous faith may cost you approval, but it gains you alignment with God's will. So don't fear resistance; let it remind you that you're moving forward. If your obedience to God stirs opposition, press on—you're likely right where He wants you to be.

Since you are my rock and my fortress, for the sake of your name lead and guide me.

PSALM 31:3 NIV

Leading others takes courage. Knowing the right decision is usually easy. Making the right decision is hard.

JOHN C. MAXWELL

Do not follow where the path may lead. Follow God, instead, to where there is no path and leave a trail.

POWER UP

Have you ever faced opposition to your obedience to God?

TAKE A STAND

---

*The hottest places in Hell are reserved
for those who, in time of great moral crisis,
maintain their neutrality.*

I n moments of moral crisis, silence is not safety
— it's surrender. Faith was never meant to be
passive; it calls us to stand, speak, and act
even when it's uncomfortable. Jesus did not remain
neutral in the face of sin, oppression, or spiritual
need — He intervened boldly, He confronted com-
passionately, He sacrificed humbly. Today, may we
have the courage to reflect His boldness, refusing
to sit on the sidelines when truth, compassion, and
righteousness are at stake.

Why not go out on a limb? Isn't that where the fruit is?

FRANK SCULLY

Commit thy way unto the Lord; trust also in him;
and he shall bring it to pass.

PSALM 37:5

Leading followers is fast and easy, and it has little return;
leading leaders is slow and hard, and it has a great re-
turn.

JOHN C. MAXWELL

POWER UP

Where have you been neutral where you should be taking a stand?

SACRED WORK

People who never do any more than they get paid for,
never get paid for any more than they do.

ELBERT HUBBARD

This quote speaks to the heart of going the extra mile — not for applause, but as a reflection of godly character. In a culture that often settles for the bare minimum, followers of Christ are called to a higher standard: to serve with excellence, integrity, and joy, even when no one is watching. Choose today to give more than is expected, not for a paycheck, but as a quiet offering to the One who gave everything for you.

Whatever you do, work at it with all your heart, as work-ing for the Lord, not for human masters, since you know that you will receive an inheritance from the Lord as a reward. It is the Lord Christ you are serving.

COLOSSIANS 3:23-24 NIV

Winner concentrate on winning;
losers concentrate on getting by.

JOHN C. MAXWELL

People who live for themselves are in
a mighty small business.

POWER UP

What is a step up you could make at your place of work?

BUILDING UP,
NOT TEARING DOWN

Keep away from people who belittle your ambitions. Small people always do that, but the really great make you feel that you, too, can become great.

MARK TWAIN

The people we surround ourselves with have a powerful influence on our faith, vision, and purpose. Blatant discouragement often comes from those who are limited by fear, while encouragement flows from those who walk in confidence and humility. Scripture says, "*Therefore encourage one another and build each other up...*" (1 Thessalonians 5:11). God places encouragers in our lives to remind us who we are and who we're becoming in Him. Choose to walk with those who speak life into your calling and challenge you to grow — not shrink.

Consider how hard it is to change yourself and you'll understand what little chance you have of trying to change others.

JACOB M. BRAUDE

Beloved, let us love one another: for love is of God; and every one that loveth is born of God, and knoweth God.

1 JOHN 4:7

Loving people precedes leading them. People don't care how much you know until they know how much you care.

JOHN C. MAXWELL

POWER UP

What voices do you currently surround yourself with?

BETTER OR BITTER

*The difficulties of life are intended
to make us better—not bitter.*

Life's hardships can either harden our hearts or deepen our character—the choice is ours. God Himself doesn't inflict His children with suffering, but through Him the pain we experience on this side of eternity can be turned around to shape us for the better. Bitterness looks inward and backward, but faith looks upward and forward. When we surrender our struggles to God, He transforms them into tools for growth, compassion, and strength.

Consider it pure joy, my brothers and sisters, whenever you face trials of many kinds, because you know that the testing of your faith produces perseverance.

JAMES 1:2–3 NIV

Hurting people hurt other people. Once you learn this, it's easier to "turn the other cheek."

JOHN C. MAXWELL

Life doesn't do anything to you. It only reveals your spirit.

POWER UP

Do you have any residual bitterness that is holding you back from growth?

GROWING FORWARD

This bold question challenges us to reflect on whether we're truly growing or just getting by. God never intended for us to live in spiritual stagnation—He calls us from glory to glory, always inviting us into deeper transformation. That means today's version of you isn't the final one. There's still more grace to receive, more healing to experience, more purpose to walk in. Lean into God's refining process and ask Him to keep stretching, shaping, and strengthening you.

. . . I gave them this command: Obey me, and I will be your God and you will be my people. Walk in obedience to all I command you, that it may go well with you. But they did not listen or pay attention . . . They went backward and not forward.

JEREMIAH 7:23-24 NIV

If you need the people, you can't lead the people. A codependent relationship seldom grows or moves forward.

JOHN C. MAXWELL

A rut is a grave with both ends knocked out.

POWER UP

What does spiritual growth look like in your life?

WHOLEHEARTED DISCIPLESHIP

> *Men will never cast away their dearest pleasures upon the drowsy request of someone who does not even seem to mean what he says.*

I f we hope to influence others, our lives must reflect the urgency, conviction, and passion of what we believe. Jesus didn't whisper truth timidly—He lived and spoke with bold, sacrificial love. Revelation 3:16 warns, *"Because you are lukewarm —neither hot nor cold—I am about to spit you out of my mouth."* True discipleship is compelling because it's wholehearted. People are moved not by half-hearted words, but by lives on fire with purpose. If we want others to lay down lesser things for Christ, we must first show them by example that He's worth everything.

Tell me and I forget, teach me and I may remember,
involve me and I learn.

BENJAMIN FRANKLIN

The fear of the Lord is the beginning of knowledge:
but fools despise wisdom and instruction.

PROVERBS 1:7

Every change in human attitude must come through internal understanding and acceptance. Man is the only known creature who can reshape and remold himself by altering his attitude.

JOHN C. MAXWELL

POWER UP

What topic could you disciple someone in
from the experience of your life?

_____

_____

_____

_____

_____

SEIZE THE DAY

Time itself carries no agenda, it simply passes. But what we do with it determines whether it becomes our ally or our regret. This quote reminds us that time is a gift from God, and Scripture urges us to "*make the most of every opportunity, because the days are evil*" (Ephesians 5:16). Every moment holds the potential to invest in eternity, to speak life, to pursue purpose, and to grow in Christ. If we wait for ideal conditions, we may never move—but if we seize each day with faith and intention, we can turn even the ordinary into something holy. Today is not just another page on the calendar—it's an opportunity. Use it well.

Essentially there are two actions in life. Performance and excuses. Make a decision as to which you will accept for yourself.

STEPHEN BROWN

I have seen something else under the sun: The race is not to the swift or the battle to the strong, nor does food come to the wise or wealth to the brilliant or favor to the learned; but time and chance happen to them all.

ECCLESIASTES 9:11 NIV

The leader's growth determines the people's growth.

JOHN C. MAXWELL

POWER UP

What "ideal conditions" have you delaying action?

LIVING ON PURPOSE

W ishes are passive, but purpose is powerful—and in Christ, we are called not just to dream, but to live with intentional direction. When we surrender our desires to God and walk in His will, our lives gain focus, energy, and spiritual significance. Faith is so much more than wishful thinking—seek His purposes, and pursue it with boldness.

Never give up, for that is just the place and time that the tide will turn.

HARRIET BEECHER STOWE

Watch your life and doctrine closely. Persevere in them, because if you do, you will save both yourself and your hearers.

1 TIMOTHY 4:16 NIV

It's lonely at the top . . . so you'd better know why you're there.

JOHN C. MAXWELL

POWER UP

What new step could you take to live with purpose?

COMMITTING TO PROGRESS

Excellence is the gradual result of always striving to do better.

PAT RILEY

E xcellence isn't about perfection, it's about consistent growth. This quote reminds us that greatness is rarely achieved in a single moment, but through daily decisions to improve, refine, and press forward. When we give God our best, even in the small things, we become people of integrity, purpose, and impact. Today, don't aim for perfection—aim to be faithful in your progress.

A good heart is better than all the heads in the world.

EDWARD BULWER-LYTTON

. . . we also glory in our sufferings, because we know that suffering produces perseverance; perseverance, character; and character, hope. And hope does not put us to shame, because God's love has been poured out into our hearts through the Holy Spirit, who has been given to us.

ROMANS 5:3-5 NIV

It's wonderful when the people believe in their leader; it's more wonderful when the leader believes in the people.

JOHN C. MAXWELL

POWER UP

What commitment can you make to progress today?

OVERFLOW OF THE HEART

*Only the person who has faith in himself
is able to be faithful to others.*

ERICH FROMM

True faithfulness to others begins with a deep sense of identity rooted in Christ. When we believe we are who God says we are—beloved, chosen, and equipped—we're able to pour into others with consistency and strength. Confidence overflows into encouraging relationships, steady leadership, and authentic servanthood. Believe in who God made you to be and, from the overflow of your heart, aid others you're currently sharing a path with.

Learning what you cannot do is more important than knowing what you can do.

LUCILLE BALL

We love because he first loved us.

1 JOHN 4:19 NIV

Leadership functions on the basis of trust. When trust is gone, the leader soon will be.

JOHN C. MAXWELL

POWER UP

What is overflowing from your heart in this current season of life?

_____

_____

_____

_____

_____

THE LENS OF FAITH

Nothing is as hard as it looks; everything is more rewarding than you expect; and if anything can go right it will and at the best possible moment.

JOHN C. MAXWELL

This quote is a beautiful reminder that faith reframes our perspective: what initially feels overwhelming can become manageable, what seems uncertain can yield unexpected joy, and what feels delayed can arrive in perfect timing. When we trust God's timing and provision, we begin to see challenges not as dead ends but as doorways to greater reward. Keep going, even when it's hard — the best things often come when you least expect.

Ninety percent of the work done in this country is done by people who don't feel well.

THEODORE ROOSEVELT

And we know that all things work together for good to them that love God, to them who are the called according to his purpose.

ROMANS 8:28

Attitude is a choice. Happiness is a choice. Optimism is a choice. Kindness is a choice. Giving is a choice. Respect is a choice. Whatever choice you make makes you. Choose wisely.

ROY T. BENNETT

POWER UP

What lens filters your outlook on life?

STRENGTH TRAINING

Difficulties mastered are opportunities won.

WINSTON CHURCHILL

E very challenge we face is more than an obstacle — it's an invitation to grow, to trust, and to rise. When we persevere through trials, we don't just survive, we gain ground. God is not ignorant to our struggles; He can use them to shape us into people of endurance, wisdom, and faith if we let Him. When you shift your perspective to seeing difficulty as strength training, you'll discover the diamonds hidden within.

He that is of a proud heart stirreth up strife: but he that putteth his trust in the Lord shall be made fat.

PROVERBS 28:25

People buy into the leader before they buy into the leader's vision. If you want to lead, you must sell yourself.

JOHN C. MAXWELL

Commitment in the face of conflict produces character.

POWER UP

What difficulty have you faced that you now credit as strength training?

OWNING UP

*Anyone who has made a mistake
and doesn't correct it, is making another one.*

E verybody makes mistakes, but refusing to correct them is detrimental in more ways than one. Humility and repentance are not signs of weakness, they are the foundations of wisdom. God doesn't expect perfection from us or He wouldn't have needed to send His Son! But He does call us to turn back, learn, and move forward renewed. Don't fear course correction — embrace it, and find freedom on the other side.

Whoever conceals their sins does not prosper, but the one who confesses and renounces them finds mercy.

PROVERBS 28:13 NIV

Admit your failures quickly and humbly. The people already know when you've erred, but they'll appreciate your right spirit.

JOHN C. MAXWELL

You never have to recover from a good start.

POWER UP

What course correction do you need to make?

_____

_____

_____

_____

_____

NEVER SURRENDER

The harder you work, the harder it is to surrender.

VINCE LOMBARDI

Perseverance deepens our resolve, not just in our own strength, but in our spiritual journey as well. When we labor diligently in faith, obedience, and prayer, giving up becomes less of an option and more of a contradiction to what we've sown. Every step of faithful effort makes surrendering to fear, doubt, or discouragement harder to justify. Keep pressing on, not just to finish strong, but because God has already won the victory on our behalf.

Persistence is stubbornness with a purpose.

RICH DEVOS

From the fruit of their lips people are filled with good things, and the work of their hands brings them reward.

PROVERBS 12:14 NIV

Never take shortcuts. They don't pay off in the long run.

JOHN C. MAXWELL

POWER UP

What ground have you given up in your life that God is calling you to take back?

_____

_____

_____

_____

_____

A LEAP OF FAITH

There's no halfway when it comes to trusting God. Like Peter stepping out of the boat, or Abraham leaving everything familiar, true breakthroughs often come when we take courageous, all-in leaps. When God calls you to cross a chasm—whether it's a new calling, a hard decision, or a deep surrender—He's asking for your trust. Take the leap, because when your faith is in Him, He will meet you midair.

Read the best books first, or you may not have a chance to read them at all.

HENRY DAVID THOREAU

The Lord is my portion, saith my soul; therefore will I hope in him.

LAMENTATIONS 3:24

Where there is no hope in the future, there is no power in the present.

JOHN C. MAXWELL

POWER UP

What big leap have you been hesitating on taking?

_____

_____

_____

_____

_____

LIFE UNDER THE SURFACE

God never puts anyone in a place too small to grow.

Sometimes we find ourselves in seasons that feel hidden, limited, or insignificant—but this quote reminds us that God knows what He's doing. Like a seed planted in soil, our growth often begins where no one sees. Zechariah 4:10 says, *"Do not despise these small beginnings, for the Lord rejoices to see the work begin."* Whether you're in a quiet job, a humble role, or a waiting season, trust that God is cultivating purpose and strength in you. Don't measure your potential by your surroundings; measure it by the God who placed you there.

Christians are supposed not merely to endure change, nor even profit by it, but to cause it.

HARRY EMERSON FOSDICK

Do not conform to the pattern of this world, but be transformed by the renewing of your mind. Then you will be able to test and approve what God's will is—his good, pleasing and perfect will.

ROMANS 12:2 NIV

I teach what I know, but I reproduce what I am.

JOHN C. MAXWELL

POWER UP

What might God be trying to grow in you right now, even in a place or season that feels small or insignificant?

THE COMPANY YOU KEEP

*Your friends will stretch your vision
or choke your dream.*

The people we choose to surround ourselves with either breathe life into our God-given dreams or quietly drain the courage we need to pursue them. God often uses others to sharpen us, encourage us, and stir our faith—but He also calls us to discernment. Friends who stretch your vision will challenge you to grow, believe, and obey God more fully. Choose companions who lift your eyes to what God can do and be that kind of friend in return.

A friend loves at all times, and a brother is born for a time of adversity.

PROVERBS 17:17 NIV

People are your only appreciable asset.

JOHN C. MAXWELL

Look carefully at the closest associations in your life, for that is the direction you are heading.

POWER UP

Are the people you surround yourself with encouraging you to pursue God's purpose for your life?

UPSIDE DOWN KINGDOM

Life is a lot like tennis—the one who can serve best seldom loses.

God's kingdom is not like ours: greatness is measured not by how much we gain, but by how well we serve. Jesus said, *"Whoever wants to become great among you must be your servant"* (Matthew 20:26). The world may chase status, but God honors the humble heart that gives, encourages, and lifts others up. When we make service our posture—at home, at work, in our communities—we reflect the heart of Jesus.

*The measure of a life, after all, is not its duration
but its donation.*

CORRIE TEN BOOM

*And whosoever of you will be the chiefest,
shall be servant of all.*

MARK 10:44

*Leadership is servanthood. Observance of this truth keeps
your motives pure and protects you from ambition. It also
makes you like Jesus.*

JOHN C. MAXWELL

POWER UP

How might a heart of service lead to greater impact and fulfillment?

THE TRUE MEASURE OF LIFE

When God measures man, he puts the tape around his heart, not his head.

While the world may measure success by intellect, status, or outward appearance, God looks deeper. It's not our cleverness or credentials that impress Him, but our a humble, obedient heart. God desires hearts that are surrendered, teachable, and aligned with His. So today, don't strive to merely appear right — strive to be right in heart. Because in God's eyes, the true measure of greatness is love.

If you think you can, you can.
And if you think you can't, you're right.

MARK KAY ASH

But the Lord said to Samuel, "Do not consider his appear-
ance or his height, for I have rejected him. The Lord does
not look at the things people look at. People look at the out-
ward appearance, but the Lord looks at the heart."

1 SAMUEL 16:7 NIV

Problems are not our problems. It's not what happens to
you but what happens in you that matters.

JOHN C. MAXWELL

POWER UP

Are you more focused on growing in knowledge
or in cultivating a heart that reflects God's character?

FAILURE IS A FORGE

---

*Experience is knowing a lot of things
you shouldn't do.*

WILLIAM KNUDSON

Much of what we call wisdom is forged through a series of errors, slip-ups, and skinned knees. Thankfully, failure is not the end of the story. The wrong choices, the closed doors, the painful consequences — they all become part of the refining process when we surrender them to God. Don't be ashamed of the lessons learned the hard way. Let them shape your character, sharpen your discernment, and deepen your dependence on the Author of our faith.

The young man knows the rules,
but the old man knows the exceptions.

OLIVER WENDELL HOLMES

Where is the wise person? Where is the teacher of the law?
Where is the philosopher of this age? Has not God made
foolish the wisdom of the world?

1 CORINTHIANS 1:20 NIV

Most people are educated way beyond their level
of obedience.

JOHN C. MAXWELL

POWER UP

How has God used your past mistakes to teach you wisdom?

THE RISK OF PROGRESS

Progress in life and faith always requires movement—and movement involves risk. We can't move forward while clinging to the safety of where we've been. Just like a base runner must leave first to reach second, we must be willing to step out in faith, even when the outcome isn't guaranteed. If you sense God nudging you forward, don't let fear cement your feet. Trust that He's already there waiting at second base.

All life is the management of risk, not its elimination.

WALTER WRISTON

*The plans of the diligent lead to profit
as surely as haste leads to poverty.*

PROVERBS 21:5 NIV

Timing is everything. The right setup will keep an organization from having a wrong setback.

JOHN C. MAXWELL

POWER UP

What fear or comfort are you holding onto that might be keeping you from the next stage of growth God has for you?

HEEDING THE CALL

The difference between what we do and what we are capable of doing would suffice to solve most the world's problems.

MAHATMA GANDHI

This quote challenges us to examine the gap between our comfort zone and our God-given capacity. So often, we settle for doing "just enough," when God has placed within us far more potential than we dare to use. Ephesians 2:10 reminds us, *"For we are God's handiwork, created in Christ Jesus to do good works, which God prepared in advance for us to do."* The world aches for hope, justice, compassion, and truth — and much of what it needs lies dormant in the hearts of believers who haven't yet stepped fully into their calling. Ask God to awaken in you the courage to heed His call.

*If we did all the things we are capable of doing,
we would literally astonish ourselves.*

THOMAS EDISON

*He hath shewed thee, O man, what is good; and what doth
the Lord require of thee, but to do justly, and to love mercy,
and to walk humbly with thy God?*

MICAH 6:8

*To lead others to do right is wonderful. To do right
and then lead them is more wonderful . . . and harder.*

JOHN C. MAXWELL

POWER UP

*Am I fully using the gifts, opportunities, and potential God has given
me or am I settling for less than what He's called me to do?*

CLINGING TO HOPE

Determination is more than sheer will-power — it's faith in action when the road runs out. Galatians 6:9 encourages us, "*Let us not become weary in doing good, for at the proper time we will reap a harvest if we do not give up.*" God doesn't ask us to have all the answers, just the courage to keep trusting Him when nothing makes sense. That knot at the end of your rope might be your last hope that holds you steady. Don't give up. What looks like the end might just be the moment God is about to move.

Above all, try something.

FRANKLIN D. ROOSEVELT

Blessed is the one who perseveres under trial because, having stood the test, that person will receive the crown of life that the Lord has promised to those who love him.

JAMES 1:12 NIV

God chooses what we go through;
we choose how we go through it.

JOHN C. MAXWELL

POWER UP

What keeps you going in hard times?

_____

_____

_____

_____

_____

NOT CALLED TO AVERAGE

> *Nobody gets to run the mill by doing*
> *run-of-the-mill work.*
>
> **THOMAS J. FRYE**

God didn't create you for mediocrity — He crafted you for excellence with purpose and passion. He honors wholehearted effort, not just in grand achievements, but in daily faithfulness. Whether you're building a business, raising a family, or serving in unseen ways, doing your best for His glory sets you apart. Give God your best, and He will give you His best.

You have to give up to go up.

DAVID JEREMIAH

A good name is rather to be chosen than great riches, and loving favour rather than silver and gold.

PROVERBS 22:1

Respect is vital to a leader. Without it, no one follows. Title or position will not help it. With it, everyone follows, and title or position are not needed.

JOHN C. MAXWELL

POWER UP

What can you do today that goes beyond the ordinary—something that reflects excellence, passion, and faithfulness in the work God has given you?

IDEAL GROWING CONDITIONS

I make progress by having people around me who are smarter than I am—and listening to them. And I assume that everyone is smarter about something than I am.

HENRY KAISER

T rue growth begins with humility — the kind that recognizes wisdom doesn't always come from within, but often through the people God places around us. When we stop trying to prove we know it all and start listening with a teachable heart, God uses the insight of others to sharpen us, guide us, and open our eyes to what we couldn't see alone. Everyone has something to teach us, if we're willing to listen. Surround yourself with wisdom, and you'll find that growth isn't just possible — it's inevitable.

Progress is a tide. If we stand still we will surely be drowned. To stay on the crest, we have to keep moving.

HAROLD MAYFIELD

Plans are established by seeking advice; so if you wage war, obtain guidance.

PROVERBS 20:18 NIV

Those closest to the leader determine his level of success or failure. Mentoring potential leaders insures the leader and the organization of reaching their potential.

JOHN C. MAXWELL

POWER UP

Are you surrounding yourself with wise people, and more importantly, are you humbly listening and learning from them?

STICK IT OUT

> *My God-given talent is my ability to stick with something longer than anyone else.*
>
> **HERSCHEL WALKER**
> **HEISMAN TROPHY WINNER**

I n a world that celebrates quick wins and instant results, this quote reminds us that perseverance is a powerful, God-given gift. Sticking with something when others give up isn't just grit—it's faith in motion. Endurance is often the difference between giving up and growing into the person God designed you to be. If your strength lies in showing up day after day, even when it's hard, don't underestimate it—that's a holy calling. God sees your faithfulness, and He always finishes what He starts.

A great man stands on God.

RALPH WALDO EMERSON

*The Lord is my rock, and my fortress, and my deliverer;
my God, my strength, in whom I will trust; my buckler,
and the horn of my salvation, and my high tower.*

PSALM 18:2

*The gift is greater than the leader. God's anointing upon
our lives points to His greatness, not ours.*

JOHN C. MAXWELL

POWER UP

When things get tough, where or who do you turn to first?

CALLED TO NEW HEIGHTS

Never, never stop growing. Plateaus should only be found in geography books, not in personal experience.

In God's Kingdom, there's no retirement from transformation—only deeper maturity, fuller surrender, and greater purpose. Plateaus are spiritual signals to climb higher. God is never done shaping you, teaching you, or using you. Don't settle for where you are. The more you grow, the more room He has to work through you.

*One who gains strength by overcoming obstacles possesses
the only strength which can overcome adversity.*

ALBERT SCHWEITZER

*. . . "'You have been faithful with a few things;
I will put you in charge of many things.
Come and share your master's happiness!'"*

MATTHEW 25:21 NIV

*Leading people is a responsibility, not a perk.
To whomever much is given, much is required.*

JOHN C. MAXWELL

POWER UP

How do you break out of a period of plateau?

TAKE HEART

L ife's outcomes are often shaped less by what happens to us and more by the attitude we carry through it all. Jesus prepares us for hardship with these words of encouragement in John 16:33: *"I have told you these things, so that in me you may have peace. In this world you will have trouble. But take heart! I have overcome the world."* A heart anchored in faith sees setbacks as setups, pain as growth, and challenges as opportunities. Choose to live like an overcomer today.

*To err is human . . . but when the eraser wears out ahead
of the pencil, you're overdoing it.*

JERRY JENKINS

*My flesh and my heart faileth: but God is the strength of
my heart, and my portion for ever.*

PSALM 73:26

*Jesus is my best friend. At times I have failed people.
At times people have failed me. Jesus never fails.*

JOHN C. MAXWELL

POWER UP

*When faced with challenges, are you choosing a mindset of faith or
letting circumstances dictate your attitude and outlook?*

FAILURE TO THRIVE

There are a lot of ways to become a failure,
but never taking a chance is the most successful.

T he greatest failure isn't falling short — it's
never stepping out at all. God has not
called us to a life of comfort, but of
courageous obedience. Playing it safe may protect
us from mistakes, but it also robs us of miracles.
Faith takes risks — not reckless leaps, but bold steps
led by trust in your holy Guide. Don't let fear of
failure keep you from living the life God designed
for you.

*Life is like a taxi. The meter just keeps a-ticking whether
you are getting somewhere or just standing still.*

LOU ERICKSON

Therefore, since we have such a hope, we are very bold.

2 CORINTHIANS 3:12 NIV

You are only an attitude away from success!

JOHN C. MAXWELL

POWER UP

*What step of faith have you been avoiding out of fear and what
might God do if you finally take that chance?*

LIVING FOR ETERNITY

> *Make sure the thing you're living for*
> *is worth dying for.*
>
> **CHARLES MAYS**

No one wants to look back at their life and face the question of what they did with the time they were given with regret. How many little feelings we dismiss in everyday life are actually nudges from God to consider the eternal scope of our lives—to live faithfully in the moment while we can? Don't waste your days chasing what fades. When your purpose is anchored in Him—loving God, serving others, advancing His Kingdom—you're not just living well, you're living for what truly matters.

Keep this Book of the Law always on your lips; meditate on it day and night, so that you may be careful to do everything written in it. Then you will be prosperous and successful.

JOSHUA 1:8 NIV

Success isn't accumulating possessions, wealth, or power. Success is obeying God. It means having those closest to you love and respect you the most.

JOHN C. MAXWELL

People will work eight hours a day for pay, ten hours a day for a good boss, and twenty-four hours a day for a good cause!

POWER UP

Is your purpose anchored in eternal significance or do you find yourself peoccupied with short-term goals?

LIVING LARGE

When Jesus spoke of the Kingdom of God, He used words like abundance, greatness, and harvest, not minimums, margins, or mediocrity. Yet too often, we limit God by our fear, doubt, or small thinking. Ephesians 3:20 says He is able to do *"immeasurably more than all we ask or imagine."* This isn't to say that you need to become president to fulfill the calling of God, but live life aware of the ripple effects of our actions. Spread kindness and truth as you live your life, not belittling your efforts, but with faith that the impact in much larger than you can imagine.

And he said, "The things which are impossible with men are possible with God."

LUKE 18:27

See your people as they could be, not as they are.

JOHN C. MAXWELL

When someone puts a limit on what you will do, that person has put a limit on what you can do.

POWER UP

Have you minimized any part of Christ's calling on your life?

_____

_____

_____

_____

_____

GETTING WISER
BY THE DAY

---

*Don't think much of a person who is not wiser today
than he was yesterday.*

This quote challenges us to view each day as an invitation to grow in wisdom. God never intended for us to live on spiritual autopilot. He desires that we mature in grace, truth, and understanding daily. Proverbs 4:7 tells us, *"Wisdom is supreme – so get wisdom. And whatever else you get, get understanding."* Life isn't just about surviving another 24 hours; it's about becoming more like Christ through each experience, success, or struggle. Keep your heart open and your spirit teachable, because growth is the fruit of godly wisdom pursued one day at a time.

Most of the things worth doing in the world had been de-clared impossible before they were done.

LOUIS D. BRANDEIS

Teach me to do your will, for you are my God; may your good Spirit lead me on level ground.

PSALM 143:10 NIV

The next time you go looking for a book written by an ex-pert, find out if the author's ever actually done what he's proposing.

JOHN C. MAXWELL

POWER UP

What evidence of growth do you see in how you live and lead today compared to years past?

LIVE WITH PURPOSE, NOT JUST PLANS

Most people spend more time planning Christmas than they do planning their lives.

Budgeting for gifts, planning meals, booking flights, clearing bedrooms for visiting family, decorating the house from head to toe, and icing a hundred sugar cookies — Christmas can be a lot of work! While traditions and holidays matter, God calls us to live with daily intention, not just seasonal preparation. Our lives are meant to reflect more than fleeting moments, they're designed to carry eternal impact. What if we gave our life's purpose the same thought, prayer, and focus we give to holidays? Every day counts in the short time we have on this earth.

*Very often a change of self is needed more
than a change of scene.*

BENSON

*May the God who gives endurance and encouragement
give you the same attitude of mind toward each other that
Christ Jesus had . . .*

ROMANS 15:5 NIV

The attitude of your people is a reflection of your attitude.

JOHN C. MAXWELL

POWER UP

*Are you investing the same care, intention, and prayer into planning your
life with God's purpose in mind as you do into temporary celebrations?*

GLIDE ABOVE THE NOISE

When the eagles are silent, the parrots begin to jabber.

WINSTON CHURCHILL

In a world overwhelmed by opinions, distractions, and surface-level noise, we're called to be people of depth, discernment, and bold truth. Proverbs 17:27 says, *"The one who has knowledge uses words with restraint, and whoever has understanding is even-tempered."* Eagles fly with intentionality, calculation, and elegance. Likewise, godly wisdom listens carefully and speaks when it matters. Don't let the noise of the world drown out your calling. Stay close to God and rise above the noise with the quiet strength of those who wait on the Lord.

A wise man will hear, and will increase learning; and a man of understanding shall attain unto wise counsels . . .

PROVERBS 1:5

Pastors shouldn't preach another sermon until the people they lead do what they've been asked to do in the last one.

JOHN C. MAXWELL

Often a leader's greatest challenge is dealing with the multitudes of people oblivious to the obvious.

POWER UP

How do you manage "noise" in your life?

EVERLASTING REWARD

World records are only borrowed.

SEBASTIAN COE
BRITISH MIDDLE-DISTANCE RUNNER

T his quote is a humbling reminder that no matter how great our achievements, they are temporary. Records are made to be broken, but a life lived for Christ leaves an eternal legacy. 1 Corinthians 9:25 says, *"Everyone who competes in the games goes into strict training. They do it to get a crown that will not last, but we do it to get a crown that will last forever."* Pursuing excellence is good, but true greatness isn't measured by trophies or titles —it's measured by faithfulness, character, and the lives we touch.

If something has been done a particular way for fifteen or twenty years, it's a pretty good sign, in these changing times, that it is being done the wrong way.

ELLIOT M. ESTES

. . . for all have sinned and fall short of the glory of God . . .

ROMANS 3:23 NIV

The question is not "Are you going to fail?" The questions is, "How are you going to handle your failure?"

JOHN C. MAXWELL

POWER UP

What reward drives you day-to-day?

_____

_____

_____

_____

_____

A WORTHY CHALLENGE

If at first you do succeed, try something harder.

There are few things as satisfying as accomplishing a goal you've worked hard for. While savoring a victory is sweet, success is not the finish line — it's often an invitation to climb higher. When God gives you victory, it's not to make you complacent but to prove He can be trusted with the next challenge. He challenges us to keep stretching, growing, and daring beyond what's comfortable. So if you've succeeded, thank God, and then ask Him what mountain He wants you to climb next.

Success in life comes not from holding a good hand,
but in playing a poor hand well.

DENIS WAITLEY AND REM L. WITT

And I will bring the third part through the fire, and will
refine them as silver is refined, and will try them as gold
is tried: they shall call on my name, and I will hear them:
I will say, "It is my people," and they shall say, "The Lord
is my God."

ZECHARIAH 13:9

Life is not a dress rehearsal.

JOHN C. MAXWELL

POWER UP

What area of your life could you kick up a notch?

STAYING ROOTED

We are living in days of change. My grandfather had a farm. My father had a garden. But I've got a can opener.

In the trade-off between striving and convenience, there is a degree of beauty lost in the process. While change is inevitable, it's vital we don't lose what truly sustains us—deep roots in faith, discipline, and gratitude. Jeremiah 6:16 says, "*Stand at the crossroads and look; ask for the ancient paths, ask where the good way is, and walk in it, and you will find rest for your souls.*" In a world that values speed over substance, we must remember the richness of hard work, prayerful living, and dependence on God. Let's not settle for spiritual shortcuts. Dig deep.

And he said: "Truly I tell you, unless you change and become like little children, you will never enter the kingdom of heaven."

MATTHEW 18:3 NIV

Get a life of your own. Where's the joy in inheriting someone else's?

JOHN C. MAXWELL

We cannot become what we need to be by remaining what we are.

POWER UP

In a world of increasing convenience, are you still cultivating the values of faith, hard work, and intentional living?

ON TO MATURITY

> *If in the last few years you haven't discarded a major opinion or acquired a new one, check your pulse. You may be dead.*
>
> **GELETT BURGESS**

You're not the same person you were a year ago. You're not even the same person you were two weeks ago, scientists report. Human skin cells completely regenerate in the span of two to four weeks. Why would our spiritual and thought life be any different? A living faith doesn't cling stubbornly to old assumptions or pridefully resist change; it listens, learns, and lets the Holy Spirit shape its convictions. If your walk with God looks exactly the same as it did years ago, it may be time to ask: Am I still growing?

Any business or industry that pays equal rewards to its goof-offs and its eager-beavers sooner or later will find itself with more goof-offs than eager-beavers.

MIKE DELANEY

The righteous is more excellent than his neighbour: but the way of the wicked seduceth them.

PROVERBS 12:26

"Average" has become so bad that a person can just show up to go to the head of the class.

JOHN C. MAXWELL

POWER UP

What belief, habit, or mindset might God be prompting you to reexamine or surrender so you can grow deeper in maturity?

STOCKHOLM SYNDROME

---

*Most people are more comfortable with old problems
than with new solutions.*

S ometimes we cling to the comfort of old struggles rather than embrace the uncertainty of
new freedom. The Israelites in Exodus longed
for Egypt even after God had miraculously delivered
them — proof that familiarity can feel safer than trusting God. But Isaiah 43:19 reminds us of His voice:
*"See, I am doing a new thing! Now it springs up; do you
not perceive it?"* God's solutions often stretch us, challenge us, and lead us into the unknown, but they also
heal, restore, and transform. Don't let fear of the un-
familiar keep you bound to what God is trying to free
you from. Step into His new thing.

Remove the dross from the silver, and a silversmith can produce a vessel . . .

PROVERBS 25:4 NIV

Growth is a process. Death may be automatic, but growth is not.

JOHN C. MAXWELL

Be willing to give up all that you now are to be all that you can become.

POWER UP

What struggle are you clinging to out of familiarity, and what step can you take to embrace a new solution God might be offering?

NO FAITH IN NEUTRALITY

> *We know what happens to people who stay in the middle of the road; they get run over.*
>
> ANEURIN BEVAN

I ndecision is a decision, and often a dangerous one. In Revelation 3:16, God says to the church in Laodicea, *"Because you are lukewarm — neither hot nor cold — I am about to spit you out of my mouth."* Faith that hesitates, compromises, or avoids commitment is not faith at all. The middle of the road might feel safe, but it's where passion dies and purpose stalls. God calls us to choose: life or death, truth or deception, bold obedience or passive delay. Don't be paralyzed by indecision, but trust that God's direction is always worth the risk.

Deliberation is the work of many men.
Action, of one alone.

CHARLES DEGAULLE

Each one should test their own actions.

GALATIANS 6:4 NIV

If you keep doing what you've always done,
you'll always get what you've always gotten.

JOHN C. MAXWELL

POWER UP

Where have you taken neutral stances that God
might be urging you into boldness?

A GIFT MEANT TO BE SHARED

---

*The average person goes to his grave
with his music still in him.*

OLIVER WENDELL HOLMES

This quote is a powerful call to live fully and fearlessly, to pour out all that God has placed within us before our time on earth is done. Your life holds a melody only you can sing — a blend of gifts, experiences, and callings uniquely crafted by God. Don't silence your purpose out of fear, doubt, or procrastination. Let today be the day you begin to live louder, love deeper, and serve boldly. The world needs your song.

Most of us must learn a great deal every day in order to keep ahead of what we forget.

FRANK A. CLARK

The thing that hath been, it is that which shall be; and that which is done is that which shall be done: and there is no new thing under the sun.

ECCLESIASTES 1:9

You cannot overestimate the unimportance of practically everything.

JOHN C. MAXWELL

POWER UP

What God-given dream, gift, or message have you been holding back and what steps can you take to start sharing it?

_____

_____

_____

_____

_____

THE POWER OF A BRAVE BEGINNING

All accomplishment comes from daring to begin.

The difference between dreams and reality is often just the decision to begin. God doesn't require perfection—He delights in obedience and faith that moves. Whether you're launching a business, mending a relationship, or pursuing a long-buried calling, don't let fear or overthinking hold you back. Start small, start scared, but start. God honors the humble beginning, because He sees a beautiful finish ahead.

Eighty percent of success is showing up.

WOODY ALLEN

Cast not away therefore your confidence, which hath great recompence of reward. For ye have need of patience, that, after ye have done the will of God, ye might receive the promise.

HEBREWS 10:35-36

Many people go far in life because someone else thought they could.

JOHN C. MAXWELL

POWER UP

What is holding you back from daring to begin?

SEE A NEED, FILL A NEED

---

*If you're looking for a big opportunity,
seek out a big problem.*

od often hides divine opportunities inside daunting problems. David didn't become a hero until he faced Goliath. Nehemiah's calling emerged from the rubble of Jerusalem's broken walls. The world may run from problems, but people of faith lean into them—trusting that where there is need, God is there. If you want to be used greatly, don't just pray for an open door; look for the need around you.

The fewer the words, the better the prayer.

MARTIN LUTHER

*In the same way, faith by itself,
if it is not accompanied by action, is dead.*

JAMES 2:17 NIV

*If you want to help others, don't just know your faith—
show your faith.*

JOHN C. MAXWELL

POWER UP

*What is a problem in your sphere of influence
that you could do something about?*

I'M ALL EARS

No man ever listened himself out of a job.

CALVIN COOLIDGE

In this modern age of social media prevalence, millions of people are shouting their thoughts and opinions from their digital soap boxes. Those who choose to be selective with their voice and choose to listen quietly instead are sometimes deemed irrelevant or "out of touch." But listening is not weakness; it's wisdom. When we listen first—at work, in relationships, in ministry—we gain insight and earn influence. God often speaks through others, but we miss it when we rush to speak or defend ourselves. Want to lead well? Love well? Grow deeper? Start by speaking less and listening more.

Everyone must row with the oars he has.

ENGLISH PROVERB

. . . give thanks in all circumstances; for this is God's will
for you in Christ Jesus.

1 THESSALONIANS 5:18 NIV

Circumstances do not make you what you are . . .
they reveal what you are!

JOHN C. MAXWELL

POWER UP

Are you a good listener? In what ways could you improve?

_____

_____

_____

_____

_____

ALREADY SATISFIED

Walk so close to God that you leave no room for the devil.

It's Thanksgiving day. You're relaxing on the couch, surrounded by people you love, with a belly full of home-cooked goodness. You turn and notice a candy dish on the side table next to you. Normally your sweet tooth would get the better of you, but after the feast you just enjoyed, the saccharine sugar bombs simply don't have the same appeal. Similarly, when we find all our satisfaction in the Lord, sin doesn't look so sweet when temptation crosses our path. The more intimately we walk with the Lord — through prayer, obedience, and worship — the less influence the devil has over our thoughts, choices, and desires. Feast of the bread of life today.

*If you don't do your homework,
you won't make your free throws.*

LARRY BIRD

For I am convinced that neither death nor life, neither angels nor demons, neither the present nor the future, nor any powers, neither height nor depth, nor anything else in all creation, will be able to separate us from the love of God that is in Christ Jesus our Lord.

ROMANS 8:38-39 NIV

Are you feeling far from God? Guess who moved?

JOHN C. MAXWELL

POWER UP

Is your spiritual diet nutritious or prone to sugary indulgences?

UNCHARTED WATERS

He who never walks except where he sees other men's tracks will make no discoveries.

This quote reminds us that following God often means stepping off the beaten path. Hebrews 11 is filled with stories of men and women who dared to walk by faith, not by sight, charting courses no one had walked before because they trusted the One who was leading them. You were not created to merely mimic the footsteps of others — you were made to seek God's unique path for your life. True discovery happens when you have the faith to step where few have gone, trusting God to guide your way.

If your horse is dead, for goodness sake—dismount!

EDDY KETCHURSID

Order my steps in thy word: and let not any iniquity have dominion over me.

PSALM 119:133

To go nowhere, follow the crowd.

JOHN C. MAXWELL

POWER UP

Where is God calling you to step out of the familiar and blaze a new trail?

_____

_____

_____

_____

_____

UNREASONABLE FAITH

> *The reasonable man adapts himself to the world; the unreasonable one persists in trying to adapt the world to himself. Therefore all progress depends on the unreasonable man.*
>
> ## GEORGE BERNARD SHAW

Real change comes not from those who settle for what is, but from those who are bold enough to pursue what could be. God often uses the "unreasonable" — those unwilling to compromise His vision — to spark revival, justice, and hope. Don't be afraid to challenge the status quo when God has called you to live set apart. Bold faith isn't always reasonable, but it always changes the world.

The world is moving so fast these days that the man who says it can't be done is generally interrupted by someone doing it.

ELBERT HUBBARD

The crucible for silver and the furnace for gold, but people are tested by their praise.

PROVERBS 27:21 NIV

People are like rubber bands: they must be stretched to be effective.

JOHN C. MAXWELL

POWER UP

Where in your life could God be asking you to stop simply adapting and instead rise up and lead change, even if it defies expectations?

_____

_____

_____

_____

_____

OPPORTUNITY CALLS

The reason so many people never get anywhere in life is because, when opportunity knocks, they are out in the backyard looking for four-leaf clovers.

WALTER P. CHRYSLER

Too many wait for perfect conditions or mysterious signs of favor, while the real open doors go unnoticed or unanswered. God is not hiding His purpose behind superstition or chance; He is inviting you to trust Him, act boldly, and step into the opportunities He places in front of you. And when you're living a diligent and godly life, they are easier to recognize. Don't miss your moment chasing luck. Faith answers the knock.

Everything comes to him who hustles while he waits.

THOMAS EDISON

The hand of the diligent shall bear rule:
but the slothful shall be under tribute.

PROVERBS 12:24

Leadership development is a lifetime journey
—not a weekend trip.

JOHN C. MAXWELL

POWER UP

Do you recognize opportunity when God places it in front of you?

WHEN GOD SHOWS UP

You have never tested God's resources until you have attempted the impossible.

T his quote is a bold invitation to live beyond our understanding and lean fully into the limitless power of God. When we only attempt what feels safe or manageable, we never truly discover the depth of His strength or the richness of His provision. But when we step into the realm of the impossible — like Peter stepping out of the boat — we give God the floor to display His glory. Do what you can with what you have, and watch Him multiply your loaves and fish.

Achievers are not only persistent, they are also hard workers who believe in themselves.

TIMOTHY L. GRIFFITH

Then he said to his disciples, "The harvest is plentiful but the workers are few. Ask the Lord of the harvest, therefore, to send out workers into his harvest field."

MATTHEW 9:37 NIV

Whiners achieve only when they feel like it. Winner achieve even when they don't.

JOHN C. MAXWELL

POWER UP

What is a time in your life that God showed up in a big way?

RUN WELL

F ocus is powerful. You could be the fastest runner on the track, but if your focus wavers from the finish line, not only could you find yourself lower on the leaderboard, but you're also robbing yourself of the joy of the journey. We're called not to compare ourselves with others, but to run the race God has uniquely set before us. You weren't made to compete with others, but to complete the mission God has given you. Run hard, run free, and keep your gaze fixed on the only One who truly matters.

He that tilleth his land shall have plenty of bread: but he that followeth after vain persons shall have poverty enough.

PROVERBS 28:19

Those who follow the crowd will never be followed by a crowd.

JOHN C. MAXWELL

The farsighted tend to get blind sighted by the nearsighted.

POWER UP

Where in your life do you need to stop comparing yourself to others?

ANCESTRAL FAITH

If we study the giants, we are less apt to be pygmies.

Scripture is full of spiritual giants — Abraham, David, Paul — whose lives of bold faith and obedience still speak to us today. Hebrews 13:7 urges, *"Remember your leaders, who spoke the word of God to you. Consider the outcome of their way of life and imitate their faith."* When we study the lives of the faithful — past and present — we gain the perspective, wisdom, and courage beyond our own. Don't settle for small thinking when God has surrounded you with examples of greatness. Learn from the great men and women of faith, and grow tall in your own calling.

You must have long-range goals to keep you from being frustrated by short-range failures.

CHARLES C. NOBLE

No discipline seems pleasant at the time, but painful. Later on, however, it produces a harvest of righteousness and peace for those who have been trained by it.

HEBREWS 12:11

Decisions are made in a moment, but growth comes from daily discipline.

JOHN C. MAXWELL

POWER UP

What spiritual giants have built you up and encouraged you in the faith?

_____

_____

_____

_____

_____

ABOUT THE AUTHOR

J ohn Maxwell is one of the world's most respected authorities on leadership and personal effectiveness. He has written more than a hundred books, including the *New York Times* best seller *The 21 Irrefutable Laws of Leadership*, which has sold more than 4 million copies. In addition to his writing career, he is a popular speaker, inspiring more than 250,000 people annually at appearances nationwide.

Dr. Maxwell's advice is based on his thirty-plus years of experience as a pastoral and organizational leader. He is founder of Maxwell Leadership, an organization that helps people maximize their personal and leadership potential. He has served as a senior pastor for churches in California, Ohio, Indiana, and Florida.

Dr. Maxwell lives in Atlanta, Georgia, with Margaret, his wife of more than fifty years.

Additional copies of this book and other titles
from Honor Books are available online.
Also available from this series:

The Power of Thinking Big
The Power of Leadership
The Power of Attitude
The Power of Influence